MY FALL AND RISE IN
BUSINESS ONLINE

*The story of an ordinary dreamer, who
still believes*

I. Introduction

My name is Victoria Mineva and I am currently in my thirties. I was born in Bulgaria. The country is in Eastern Europe and it's one of the poorest countries of the continent. Even the European Union confirmed that.

My home town is called Veliko Tarnovo. It was the old capitol of Bulgaria. Now the capitol is Sofia. Currently I live in another Bulgarian town, called Bourgas. It's a Black Sea town.

In my hometown I was involved too early with the standard society's system. On my first year I was in kindergarten, after that in school, university and then I found a daily job as employee. Everything was ok without the one thing I treasured most – my goal of to be free in every aspect. The system of the country broke few years ago my dream with my own agreement as I was hired by government employer. As you know, everything in life is about choices we make.

Since my childhood I was told I should find secure job with few days' vacation and to work from eight in the morning till five in the evening every day. This should be the life I had to live. I was told to do is this way.

The weekend days weren't always my free time. Because there was too much work I should stay late in the evenings, even till midnight and on weekends in the office. Of course, there weren't any commissions for that. I had to sacrifice my personal life and hobbies because physically I couldn't take the tire and stress. I only wanted to sleep 9 hours per night, but I couldn't.

In Bulgaria local employers want to suck all your energy and of course they don't pay you for staying late at the office or working in the weekends. Right said, the money I received as salary can guarantee me to survive, but not is not always like this. The prices for food are few times higher than in other European countries and the salaries are ten times smaller. I used for example Austrian salaries, because my check in with it is on personal interest.

I should last this way till my pension's days if I am alive then. There wasn't even a single blink of hope to climb higher in my career. I have no political connections, nor do I have the money for that. As you know, politicians everywhere are corrupt and manipulate people. In Bulgaria this is quite obvious. I don't have experience for other counties at the moment.

I did what I was told from my parents and the society in general. I should fear of losing my job I already hated. I forgot my own dreams, selling myself into Slavery of the boss's mood. I thought that I don't have the right and time to work about my wishes at all because of the hard financial situation. The living and food expenses go on every day, month and year. My routine was tight. Office and house work every single day without a time for myself. In my twenties I felt as an old hag and I looked as one in my opinion. Woman always should take care of themselves in every area of life.

I wanted to move abroad, but I didn't have the capital for that and I didn't have the time to prove my language knowledge. Most of the time I couldn't even understand the offers for jobs because as you know when a language is not spoken, it is easily forgotten.

The days went by until one Friday afternoon. My university class mate called me to go on a make-up presentation. As a woman I couldn't resist the temptation for free makeup and to know more about this field of study. On the other day in the lunchtime I began to see world in different light. I remembered a part of my dream that was long ago forgotten and buried deep inside my heart. Then I began to believe again that my life can become far better. This happened because my meeting with Network marketing industry.

II. My stories

1. Cosmetic Industry

I went of the makeup presentation that my university class mate invited me. There were three women in team and a lot of cosmetic and heath products around them. One of the women – Junior Team Leader by title presented the business model and compensation plan of the company.

The company is one of the best network marketing companies with large direct sales volume in Europe and it's German. It's established thirty years ago. German products in my opinion were only connected with the word "quality".

I was amazed by products and the stories of these three ordinary people, who reached financial freedom and traveled around the world, using quality health and beauty products. They worked on achieving their dreams and had somehow happy lives. And this was in Bulgaria? I couldn't believe it. That was unknown for me. I can say the most important part of this presentation for me was opening my own eyes for the true life outside job thinking box. I began to believe that if any other person can achieve what desires so can do I. This team really inspired me.

When the presentation ended, there was a discussion and free makeup session. I asked the women a lot of things. I could see that they were happy and confident of their lives without a boss and money worries. The makeup experience was also great for me. I didn't use eye shadows, foundation or lipstick makeup till then.

After this March day in 2011 I began to change my mind as a woman and as a dreamer, who wanted to achieve more in her life. In this year – 2011, which was emblematic for me I also became a master in Psychology .When I started first with my daily job I earned my first own salary and I invested in achieving one of my dreams – to have a MBA degree in Psychology and this came true.

I marked 2011 as the year of the beginning of my new life. It became fuller with joy and worth to be lived by following my dreams.

This Friday afternoon meeting was my first love with network marketing. I began to read all kinds of books for Multi-level Marketing and to watch all kinds of web seminars on this topic. I visited few regular seminars about networking marketing and every time I got inspired and motivated to move forward my goals.

I transformed from ordinary person with closed mind to extraordinary person with open mind. This was in my later twenties, but better later than never. I started also a blog for products of this cosmetic company and interesting stuff about network marketing.

I started to learn presenting business models and products face to face. I began to see the bright side of daily situations and routines that made me dig into depression hole before. My thinking went from deeply negative to quite positive. It was a great journey for a change of my personality. I have no regrets I transformed in a positive believer. I proved my will to become a better human being. Everyone has the will to change himself or herself only if he or she wants it for real. So, if I can do it, you can do it too.

I became happier as woman and a person with this new start of my life. I went on different presentations of another Multi-level marketing companies and I slowly began to understand what compensation plan and business model is. Most of the companies were similar in their presentations and business models. The health and beauty products always were presented as the best in the field. All of them had some certificates, so it's good to know which certificates are the most proven for the products you use.

I found out that in every business the secret is within the relationships and mutual respect. If this is amiss there is no partnership, nor is any kind of relationship. Before this emblematic meeting with this kind of business I had been forgotten about the people around myself. Every one of them has their story and accidently I found myself willing to know and support people more than usual. I didn't saw them only like whining persons with problems that should also lie on my shoulders.

- **Experience:**

My first presentation was made with the team of the tree women I joined. I invited four people – my best friend, her mother, my mother and one woman I was close to from my daily job. Not even one of these persons joined my new business. I was really disappointed, but I didn't give up. I believed in the products and I was blind for some hidden things in presentations regarding compensation plan. I was really emotionally involved with this company because it was my First, German and with great products I use till today, because they worth it.

My new team was disappointed too. I began to feel that network business it's mostly filled with rejections. I saw them as rejecting my personality, but today I see it's not like that. People are just different and are right on their path, which is not always crossed with mine. I didn't see my team again excepting one of the women two years after I joined. She was by my side on phone and skype until I stopped talking to her because of her aggressive pressure in my point of view about inviting everyone I know to presentations. I was left on my own behind sweet talk of team work and hidden things regarding business model. I found on my own later what exactly I was involved with.

My second presentation was done by myself without no one by my side. It was huge failure. I talked two hours about the products I use and not even a minute for the compensation. I didn't speak as a business woman, but as an infatuated person that is brain-washed. The person I talked to, rejected me gallantly and soon after that she deleted my coordinates from her phone and social media. I began to fall into depression. My hope for achieving my dream just went by daily tasks. But I learned something – presentations should be between fifteen and thirty minutes, no more, because become boring and that they should be explained in a simple way that makes them understandable.

My third and fourth presentations were made by one of my team members – the one that spoke often on phone with me two years after I joined the business. The presentations also were unfortunate. Soon after that I cut the talk about business with this team member and we're now just friends on social media.

People believed that this cosmetic company is scam and a pyramid that will only take their money. In reality was mostly like this regarding the financial part. You need people who buy products under your partner code every month and earn you a commission. It was more like direct sales from self-made salesman/saleswoman without own shop then network business. I summarized this after reading a lot of Multi-level marketing books and ones about personal development.

Everything for the business was made with beautiful presentation and quite inspiring words without real actions behind them. The persons in this company, who are on top are really great sellers and by my observations not even a small bit leaders. True leader doesn't talk manipulative and too much, he or she inspires the team with staying by their side in all cases. They give a hand when the partner is down or slower, this is motivation for real. Every leader is working with the workers without expecting commission and without treating the persons as "bags with money". People should respect each other and not pressure themselves.

The products of this company on the other side are really qualitied for me and my family's use. This made me stay with the company until today. I love the products, they give me self-esteem and are totally on my taste. I will use them for a very long time and they help me a lot. They're certificated with the best know certificates in the cosmetic and health industry.

When I was left on my own without a team up line I decided to make a blog and to make direct sales. As much as I received products and re-read the compensation plan I found myself not in a place to promote this kind of business using aggressive methods I saw when I went on different seminars of this company. It wasn't team building at all, but only instructive discussion how to make more sales. But there were some useful web seminars that taught me that "there is no failure, but timely stop" and "dream is a goal with deadline". That were the words of Russian top earners. I quite disagree by the way, because dream is what you live for in my opinion.

Today I am still with this company and make direct sales. I promote the products whenever I have the opportunity. I am contented I found my products to use and I am grateful that I met those three woman with the beautiful presentation that inspired me to see a new light in my life within the network marketing even if it's not with this cosmetic company. Those good stories I heard opened my imagination and I realized that I also can achieve my dream. Of course, there is too much of hard work and sacrifices. In the business there is nothing for free. My first meeting with this cosmetic company was the first step toward opening my mind box for new opportunities and truths. It is really a great journey toward developing myself better.

- **Truths for Multi-level marketing cosmetic companies that I revealed for myself and I don't like**:

a) You should make sales always and become a great even aggressive salesman/saleswoman;
b) You should say that the products are the one and only in all the

world, but they are not. It's all about the quality and world-proven certificates;

c) The business plan is not clear presented on the first presentation face to face or online – it's about catching the person's attention and taking money from him/her;

d) Is not made clear that when you have achieved a certain level to win a car and have one, you should pay leasing for it every month;

e) You should keep monthly points and invest more money to stay on the level you're. The business just doesn't give you residual income if you don't make sales every month to new people and your team doesn't buy anything;

f) There is always a big starting fee to join the networking business with cosmetic products;

g) Meet everyone without connecting with the person and make him/her to join you without any engagement to this potential new partner, who will rely on. One day you should leave him/her alone at some point;

h) Treating human beings as "bag of money" and not taking care about the person's needs;

2. Online Marketing

In the end of May 2011 I had an appointment with my best friend. Her father came with us and told me about internet business opportunity for free. At first I was really not interested to hear what he has to say because of my blindness regarding the joining of the cosmetic company. My best friend's father is in Network business from ten years and was really confident in what he told me. I listened to him later on and I decided to join the online company in June after I have read a lot of information for free.

The company was established in 1998 online, but its story began thirty years ago. There are around two millions affiliates in it already and some of them live only from earnings of the program.

People all around the world that are not so well known, but they are just ordinary persons who succeeded. In the online store for this business are over 100 000 products from all the world in all categories and 24-hours per day penny auctions where you can save up to 90% of retail price for products. I think is really good to buy cheaper. I also have sold some products and earned commissions.

- **Experience:**

When I joined the program on first of June 2011 I reached the highest possible rank and I was really inspired. When I compared the standard offline Multi-level marketing business with the online one I saw the big image and great differences. Everyone who is not in Internet, is out of the business. It doesn't matter if the business is regular or in network.

On the second month in this online business I was a rank lower, but still I haven't any commission. On my third month I received my first commission in this online business and starting then till now I have commission every single month. It's a small sum of money, but is a reward for me.

On the other side in my offline network business I only invested money in products and I didn't have a single person in my network. I made only Direct Sales and they are not every month.

Regarding my internet business I can say I learned a lot about various advertisement methods, referrals sites, traffic exchange webs and online sales. I made PayPal account and I studied a lot for payment methods in internet. I see that every month my network is growing matching my rank of Team Leader or not. Of course, there is also financial investment. If there is no investment of money, there isn't serious business.

The difference between my offline and online network business is that the re-investment of commissions bring me benefit. Every day thousands of people join this Internet opportunity in seeking for additional income option that can ensure them regular cash flow and working from home without a boss.

All the team partners in my Internet business are requited by different traffic exchange sites and referred from various places where people are really looking for an opportunity to improve their standard of living. The visitors of these sites are business seekers, not just players that want fast money.

Almost 95 % of every person that looks for an online business opportunity believes that the money somehow will fall from the sky and there is no need to work hard. The same applies for my internet business. The people who prove that they want to succeed are those whom I know from my first months in the program, when I was on highest possible level. We're together till today. Four years are a big lap of time and we became good friends through the business.

Partnership is not just for the money and mutual use, but mostly for connecting, communication and building trust in person's authority. This is the reason for me saying "Business is made with people, who communicate and share the same destination or at least a similar one"

The compensation plan in my online business is simple – inviting people, who really showed interest in what you offer, teach them what you know and show them what you buy, so they can do it too. That should be made without pressure and only when you are already connected with them. Then they will understand what and how you. The people will duplicate your shared experience and this way the strong team is already built.

This is not even a single bit close to my offline network business where I have to make a contact list and invite everyone I know even if I had no talk with him/her for years. So why should I do it this way? Why should I broke my connections or cut them with inviting them for something that they probably don't need or understand? Or they don't have money to afford it? There is no need of contact list in my opinion and it will be somewhat hypocrisy. It's better to have quiet conversations, knowing people's goals and situations. After the trust is built, there should be a story in friendly way for the business opportunity you offer. Even if I receive rejection it won't harm my current relationship with the person. The people won't feel pressured or misunderstood.

This happens only if you communicate with the heart of the person. This is what I have met in my online business. By exchanging friendly messages and e-mails I understood better person's hearts and this way I contacted the right people for my business.

What I have to do in my online business? I have to sell goods from a big online store for faster commission and achieving certain rank to build a team. I also have to play games that gives me points for a commission and share interesting information. The program supports me with everything possible that is also free for read and learn.

For the time I am in this business, I proved that I am leader to those, who are just like me and I am inspiratory for them. Our team is from leaders, not followers and true friends with similar goals.

Last month I also achieved higher rank after three years in sleeping. I had my period of desperation and giving up this great business opportunity, but today I see the full potential of it. I receive my commission that I re-invest and I am surrounded by active people, who work for their goals. They don't sit and way for a miracle to happen, nor do I. Miracles happen only if people go for them. In my opinion, for sure, there is Universe, but without action, nothing can be created.

The compensation plan of my online network marketing company is fair and clear. The benefits are given for proven results. It's easy to understand and it's also fun to do what you need to do to achieve a certain rank. In the business there are also great leaders with big income. Everything is naturally flowing.

There are not things between the dots as in my first network business company.

I learned a lot. I tried everything to see what truly works and I see my reasons being in this business clear. In it there is no need the sponsor to be by your side and make presentations for you. Everything is written in simple way. Explaining the opportunity and its compensation plan is also easy to do.

For sure it will take few more years from now to become financially independent, but my vision is clear. I will stay with this business, because it works and it's the only one I was paid for from my other network businesses activities every single month.

This year I began a new with this online business, because currently I am stay-at-home mum that takes care of her daughter. I don't want to go back to my daily job, because I want to spend more time with my baby girl and with myself working on my own life goals. But as you know the living and food expenses don't stop and I have to assure them first. After that I will think about making more money with smarter investments.

Robert Kiyosaki created the game "Cash Flow" that shows the importance of investments. When you invest in the right place you get free of loans and become financially independent. If you still haven't understand what cash flow is after reading the books of Robert Kiyosaki, try to play the game and everything will become clearer for you as it's clearer for me now.

Invest small sum of money in something you care for – business, art or something that brings benefits to you. Save 10 % from every following payment about more investment potential and after some time you will get out of loans. Then you will begin to see profits. If you can afford it, invest in real estate or shares in some stable company. In my case Network business is the most attracting choice that I can understand easily and it's cheaper option.

I invest around $100 every month in my internet business and the return of investment /ROI/ is $20. I also receive new team members. Next month's ROI will be higher. But let me tell you that money investment is not a must in my second network marketing company. There are a lot of free ways to earn commissions from my online business.

I believe that after a year or two I will stay at home and my place will be my working office. I am confident I can make this happen. In my opinion there is no need of sitting and waiting something to become reality, but only actions that are thoroughly planned and thought of are the key to successful achievement.

- **Truths about online business that I revealed for myself and I don't like:**

a) You have to work at least six hours per day for free to

advertise your gateway links on different traffic exchange sites;

b) Most of the advertisement sites on Google don't have any traffic and your ad can hardly be seen;

c) You should be great salesman/saleswoman to success in online business if you wish to become higher rank without own money investment and that means you should lie sometimes for some products just to sell them;

d) Most of the people in online business join the program and after that just disappear and you should start anew to find active team members;

e) Face to face presentation is almost impossible and that makes human contact not qualitative;

f) Big money investors take everything with their money investments in the business and the paid traffic for their gateways;

g) You can become financially independent in at least five or seven years. I mean to have really significant monthly income that covers your living expenses and gives you money in the pocket;

h) If you don't remain on certain rank you lose a part of your team;

3. Video communications

In information Era everything is going in Internet and so are the communications. Video messages, web seminars and Skype made the world global village, where you can see yourself with someone else on the other end of the world just with video camera and microphone. Let me tell you a story about my shortest streak with a Multi-level company ever.

It was 2012. I remember well this year, because it was really devastating and phoenix-rising for me. I broke my leg and had to stay at home, rooting in the bed for a month, without the ability to do even simple, daily and routine thing on my own. All the day I clicked on different traffic exchange and advertisement sites up to ten hours. I was really depressed because I couldn't go out and right said, I couldn't breathe in my current life. But I am happy that is now almost forgotten.

In this year I thought a lot about what to do with my life, where to go and how to do it. My online business was bad, my offline business was money eater. I hadn't even one active team member in both of them.

When I could step on my foot I decided to live my life at fullest and do what I really wanted to do at the moment – to visit at least one personal development seminar and to publish a book. I motivated myself to feel alive again and to move on with my living path, because I felt I did just nothing till now. I knew I should start anew.

When I visited the personal development seminar I was enlightened and inspired to do everything I can at all costs to achieve my dream – to become a richer person in all aspects /not just financially, but also emotionally/ and a writer, who changes lives only with her words of inspiration.

I had read every single book for Multi-level marketing till then and I was really attractive business partner. A lot of people tried to lure me in their companies, but I didn't like them. I felt used and I didn't see even a small bit of interest toward my personality. Every presenter just wanted to take my money. This is what I call the feeling of "a bag of money". Total amiss of simple, human communication made me doubtful toward whole Multi-level marketing business industry.

Until I met my sponsor Alex, who patiently explained to me about video communication networking business and showed concern toward my personality in every aspect. I joined him without hesitation and I met my best ever Bulgarian team members.

You know in Bulgaria most people don't like to support each other, they mostly like to drown you with themselves. The most famous motto of Bulgarians is "It's not important for me to feel alright. It's more important the others to feel bad". Yeah, these are the facts and I am not a patriot or rights offender.

Alex became my mentor in the business and we became friends. Thanks to him I learned a lot for blogging, WordPress, SEO and etc. But after almost two years I felt this video communication business is not my thing. Now I explain.

- **Experience:**

I joined the video communication business in May 2012. I was inspired for everything in it – video e-mails, video conferences, video chat and etc. Video communication can be made with Skype, which is free to use, but the quality of communication is really bad.

In my third and probably last Multi-level marketing business company there are great, quality products for video communication. For the use or them there is a monthly price and also starting price package. The possibility to feel closer to the people of the world is great known. The contact through these video products make the online meeting as real one. In the business plan there are two options:

*Making direct sales to big companies and receive commission;

* Building a team and make them pay monthly fee. Of course you should invite other people to use the platform and watch video presentation because all favors should be paid;

In short my video communication business is like "a business for the businesses". This is its concept. I really was motivated easily of our team meetings that happened every weeks for two times. But those trainings were too long and boring for me most of the time. I tried hard to invite a lot of people to daily business presentations, but only few watched them for all the time until I was involved with the business. I always explained, but unfortunately I couldn't find serious people to join the business and I didn't build my own team. I relied on my Sponsor, who placed people in my team or so called genealogy tree, because he hasn't place in his downline for them. For all the time I was in the business I didn't receive even a $1 commission. Only sweet talk how much I can earn and that I will be financially independent in ten years.

Right said, the compensation plan was really hard to understand. I also didn't see the real deal in all this stuff. I have read a few times the compensation plan and I still didn't get it. On the online presentations a lot of things were missed or not clearly explained from the plan. People didn't understood what benefit is for them to pay monthly fee for using video products with great quality. They continued to use Skype for video conferences and uploading in YouTube their clips. Today I do the same.

In the beginning I tried to explain how great is to have high quality video communications, but after some time I saw the profit for me only in recording videos, uploading them and using the platform for presentations and web seminars. It was good point, but I still had to make my videos first on my computer and after that watch them. Then I uploaded them on this platform where only people in Business and have the same platform could see my works. I made my presentation to attract potential partners outside the business wall. But they couldn't watch what I share if I didn't invite them on specific link through e-mail.

I should build e-mail contact list and to invite everyone I know on online presentations. It was similar to my offline network business and I didn't like it. I continued to use the products mostly for routine, but I didn't feel very well in doing this business. It was somehow not my thing and I began to feel it after I opened my eyes after the blindness of high stream words for motivation and sooner success which didn't come.

I participated in weekly team meetings, learned about the steps about recruiting and building team, but I didn't quite felt alright with this. It was just something like my offline business, but with video communications – face to face presentation in video, where the other person can easily be seen offline on cup of coffee if it's in your local area.

I learned a lot from this video communication business. My sponsor taught me to make blog with WordPress and to do SEO. I tried to do presentation offline when people around me were comfortable, but it didn't work well out after they have seen the online presentation. I understand it quite well.

On the other side Bulgaria is not a country where video communication is quite popular and because people are poorer they hardly can afford paying monthly fees for using video communication products that can be used for free like Skype and YouTube.

My job in this Multi-level marketing company was like this: I should record videos all the day and upload them, I should invite all my e-mail contacts on video presentations and to do web seminars through the platform to catch attention and make people join the business. I had to learn body language and how to look confident. I had to record a single video again and again for hours because of my posture for example. I should have perfect and professional expression, but not a single bit natural.

I prefer to have personal contact and see people in their eyes if they aren't far away physically. That couldn't happen with those video products although the great quality of them. I like writing e-mail to build trust more than to stay all day long before my laptop and use the video camera and microphone. In my opinion this is too much waste of time that is also limited for me.

The business model was quite unclear, but the thing I understood was that if I am on a lower price package I will receive smaller commission and if I am on the most expensive I will receive bigger one. Another disturbing thing was that: If the people under my partner code are on smallest package even if I am on the biggest one, I will receive small commission and I have to convince them to go for more expensive packages. I find this quite unfair. I became more hesitant if I joined the right business for me.

Of course there were a lot of personal meetings with my sponsor and his up line. Face to face meetings with online known colleagues always were exciting, but soon I found out that I am in this network marketing company for friendship that I could acquire through social media and for free rather than the business itself. I respect my past team members, I see them as friends, but I don't think video communications are for me. I am too conservative or probably lazy for them. I don't have motivation to move on with this network business.

One of the great things I learned from watching every web seminar when I joined this Multi-level marketing company is to see your own mistakes and make them into experience. But the most important benefit for me was that I stopped to fear of speaking in public.

This business was also my biggest failure. How it happened? Here is the answer:

It was December 2013. There should be live and online presentation in the same time about the business. It was a really big event. There should be all Bulgarian team leaders for answering guest's questions. I thought this way. I missed one of the trainings before the event. I watched the replay, but... I didn't understood quite well what exactly will be happening.

The organization of this event was made by my sponsor's lowest level partner. She was new and didn't know a lot of things. I went to her town for support. But I didn't have a single member on my own down or up line by my side. I thought I know everything that will be needed for a successful presentation and new members joining.

I went to the place where the presentation should be made and I saw that organization wasn't quite well done. There wasn't microphone and etc. In last hours before the meeting we made things better – two women with no team members on their own, knowing almost nothing really interesting for the business model and knowing the compensation plan at newbie level. What a great and courageous party you say? Yes, it was, before the people begin to ask questions which answers we didn't knew, because of the lack of experience.

The leaders showed on the screen and presented the business. Our physical presence was really strong, but not enough for a successful meeting.

The thirty people who were on the presentation watched the screen and some laughed. You know, when it comes to presenting multi-level marketing business opportunity, there should be really professional attitude and the presence of real people, who earn it's a must. When the screen presentation ended, the leaders waited for questions, but the guests felt really uncomfortable to ask someone on the projection wall. It's natural, because the only working thing in network business is one to one presentation when the persons are really connected to each other and feel comfortably in their company.

Most of the people feel ashamed to ask questions in public of other persons. The fear of public speaking is quite strong in all the world.

When the answers were given to the two persons that had the courage to ask in front of others, guests decided in silence that there will be no more questions. The connection was turned off and then the avalanche of questions to me and my partner, who were newbies with no real experience in building team with video communications business started. The questions face to face flew one after another.

We replied as much as possible, but we were not confident in our answers and this couldn't be hidden. I felt ashamed, but I took control of my emotions – I began to show what I can do with the platform, because this was the only way I could explain well what exactly video communications business is. My partner tried to answer some questions, but she wasn't too well prepared with reading the business plan. The guests felt well when saw what is possible with the video communications platform. Of course there were some remarks but in general things went smoothly.

The discussion offline was around two hours. The one online, with the upper leaders, was around twenty minutes. Big difference, right? This is because people join people, not faces online who they don't feel close to.

I felt as I am on a cross after we said byes to the guests. I saw my own lack of confidence in this business and success with it. I gave some wrong answers just because I didn't know the truth, I haven't experienced it. One thing was for sure, people felt really comfortable with me and my partner because we were before their eyes as human beings. But this wasn't enough to make our team stronger and the business model cleared. Right said, it wasn't professional at all.

This was really ***my fall*** in network marketing. I felt I am not content with this industry in general and I was deeply disappointed. I broke my relations with Bulgarian team, because I began to see things like "divide and conquer" and also some aggressive talk between my team members, who really wanted to success and earn big at all costs even not so humanistic.

In 2014 I did nothing for improving my business experience in neither one of my three Multi-level marketing businesses. I just watched some web seminars about team building and personal development.

I started my quitting of video communication industry immediately after the live presentation in December 2013. I stopped going to weekly team meetings and I just dropped out of all trainings. This video communications company wasn't for me and I felt it with all my heart. I did my business activities sometimes just because of the routine with no deeper thought. My feelings of enthusiasm, creativity and inspiration faded away.

Today I see that it is not worth to stay in Multi-level marketing business where you don't feel in right place. This way I dropped out of my first offline network business with health and cosmetic products and from the third one with video communications tools. I just do sometimes direct sales.

I feel on right place only with my second network business which is online and I know through e-mails different people from all over the world who are now in my team. I found out that is a must to be focused on only one business at time. The attention should be only on it.

- ***Truths about video communications industry I revealed on my own and don't like:***

    a) Buying the lowest package with products gives you the lowest commission and this doesn't change until you don't "upgrade" to more expensive one;

    b) Videos you upload on your own video wall can be seen only of people, who use the platform;

    c) Sending video e-mails is sent most probably in Spam folder;

    d) Slow internet connections or not so good computer equipment /microphone and camera/ and configuration kills all the pleasure of video communications that this company sell;

e) Monthly payment is in most cases lost forever from your pocket, because the ROI /return of investment doesn't happen in next ten years/;

f) The quality of recorded video doesn't change with the upload of the platform – if it's bad, it stays like this and there is no correction;

g) Auto responder gives a certain amount of e-mails and its campaigns are really hard to understand and follow;

h) Business model is similar to direct sales – you make contact list and have to convince people to buy stuff they probably don't really need /see them as "a bag of money"/;

III. Achievements

These are my stories and I don't claim I am the most successful woman in the world, but I just share my experience. I am proud and feel successful of what I have gained recent years.

In general this is my journey into Network marketing till now. I learned a lot, probably I will learn more, but at this current moment this is what I have been thorough. I don't play with words about six numbers income without hard work. The truth is that every change of living standard needs hard work and tight schedule;

This is what I am now. I became a better person and my mind opened up to a new world of opportunities. I have now bigger sight horizon in the business field. I am still not a millionaire, but I am wiser and I am sure I will be richer person in next few years.

In short my small, but own victories and achievements are these:

- Creation of a popular blog in Bulgaria for cosmetic and health products and authority in society as very good seller;
- Achieving Bronze team leader with hundreds of affiliates and residual income every month that covers investments in my own business;
- Owner of two business blogs that are popular in internet society and authority as network marketer;
- Having followers who got inspired by my words;

- Good presenter of business models, ethic's and customer's care;
- Mentor, who shows in simple way what should be done or not;

- Platform for web seminars, auto responders and SEO on my sites;
- I fought my fear to speak in public;
- Serious presence in social media;
- Self-publisher of own books;
- Steps ahead toward my goals;
- Taking action for more successful events;
- Moving away from mediocrity;
- Change of my own life for better;

IV. Strategies

What strategies I found out for my business? I won't quote people, who everyone knows and can find on my blog's articles, I will just state few things that I believe are my own strategies:

*__Communication is the key to success__ – regular communication with precious people, who won't whine if you don't call them daily. The questions that should be discussed on first meetings with new person are not about the business, but for the person's heart and situations. This is the start of connecting as human beings, because people join people. I even have a presentation on this topic.

* __Inviting people to my business from social networks__ – These days personal contact is rare, because all the people are going on with their lives – work, home, hobbies and the time is limited for themselves. They build all day

long their businesses, but forget that human beings should be treated as ones. It's really easy to unfriend someone on social media and nobody can tell you anything. The ties can be cut without a problem, but still – if you don't call real people on phone or e-mail, they will just fade away from your party and you will stay alone. Here come the social networks people's contacts. All of us are in Internet and can find new contacts if they want and spend precious time to build the relationship. This happens in few personal messages and after that comes the decision what will happen with a certain contact. I watched web seminars of popular networkers and I have built my own strategy regarding this topic. I have a presentation for this.

* ***Development of myself*** – when I started with network marketing I was shy and I feared what will tell the people if I speak them about business and my problems. Now I see that the best thing one can do is to stay human and to show his or her personal side, not just professional. When everything about you is clear and known, people trust you easier and they really see you as authority. I have some interesting articles about this on my business blogs in Bulgarian and English.

* ***Inspiration to person's lives*** – You know that most of people are disappointed and see no path in their lives. Inspire them at all costs. It doesn't matter if they join your business or not. The importance of self-belief, self-esteem and confidence is a must for every healthy relationship. Show that you really can do the things and people will be inspired from you. In my case I know a lot of people who now are successful on their own paths, just because I listened to them, shared my opinion and experience. Sincere words warm up the heart and give motivation.

* ***Simplicity*** – a lot of businessmen and women use complicated words to show they're smart. Be simple in words and act as ordinary person even if you have achieved big things. People are equal

and they just want some attention and simple explanations. I recently use simple answers "Yes" or "No". But believe me, once upon a time I used very complicated language and I gained nothing from it. Even my closest ones broken with me in their hearts. Arrogance, aggression, thinking you're bigger than others and using complicated words kills all the humanity. It leads to being alone not just in the business, but also in life. Humans are social beings and they need regular communication. For some is once or twice per month, for others - every day.

These are my "strategies" if I can call them like that. I am real and ordinary person who believes in better happenings tomorrow. I do what it takes to achieve my dreams.

V. In the end

In 2015 I began to think about my life from now on with my daughter, whom I need to take care of. I had two choices:

-To return on my daily job and work for a boss with small salary;

- To try my best to become my own chef and be financially independent.

I chose the second option, but then few questions popped up in my mind:

- ✓ How much time and money I can spend?
- ✓ How long will take to see the results?
- ✓ What actions should I take?
- ✓ What sacrifices I have to make?
- ✓ Where should I try to build successful business?
- ✓ Who will support me to go on the top?
- ✓ Who will be the people by my side there?

I thought through fully about my current situation and what I can do. My business with cosmetic and health products became just direct selling sometimes and my video communication business was time eater. I didn't feel good with them. The investments in both didn't gave me any income and I didn't have the time to do them anymore. It's true I had support when I needed it, but still it wasn't enough motivation for me to stay tuned.

My heart also was silent for both of these multi-level marketing businesses. They were not my thing and they didn't make me even a step closer to my life dreams.

In both of these network businesses there weren't any persons by my side. I didn't have a vision for these two network companies. I have read a lot and I saw that the only successful business should be in Internet.

I choose to stay in my online business that I started four years ago and abandoned it for a while. I began to do it again and I saw the profits I can gain from it in comparison with the other two. My focus went just in this multi-level company without any distractions. The investment in it also was smarter and the sacrifices I should make were smaller. This way I dropped out of my first and third Multi-level marketing businesses and I stopped my investments of time and money in them.

After my coming back in my internet company I achieved the rank of Bronze team leader and my commission become bigger. This became ***my rise*** in online business. I also found new team members, who are quite active and think similar to me.

I can see now persons by my side and I have great support of my higher level mentors, who don't call me just to tell me I do something wrong and I don't invite enough people of presentations. I am inspired to move on with this online business, because I see its worth.

Today I invest two to four hours per day into my business and around $100 every month, but I see them returning to me in different prizes and new team members. I can say this is my thing, because I don't feel pressured to do something I don't like to and I can spend time with my daughter. I also have action plan for example and I know clear when and how much I will earn. I have built residual income, which is not so significant at the moment to brag of, but I climb higher every month. This makes me closer to my dream "To stay and work from home" without thinking about living and food expenses.

Meanwhile I also do what I love to do – to write. I already published two books, this is my third.

I don't feel tired from my monthly schedule and routine as I felt in my first and third network marketing businesses. I do the things that should be done with joy. I am real person with sincere heart and people follow me for what I am, not for how professional posture I have.

This is the end of my stories. I believe my example with multi-level marketing was useful for you.

Think carefully about what you truly want and what kind of business you need for achieving it. Do you like to have contact lists and doing daily presentations? If yes, then you have the vision about being in a company like ones in my first and third network businesses. You should prepare contact lists and presentation to build your team and of course, to overcome your fear to speak in public.

If you don't like to be under the lights for presentations in public, my internet business is for you. There is no need of contact lists, the program takes care of building a team if you're on a certain rank and have made some investment.

The main point of my book is for you to listen to your heart's desire and think what is really for you. Is the network business for you or not? Are you successful or not? My definition of success is "doing something you love without feeling tired and pressured". It's good to have a smart action plan for your own needs, but if you don't have in the beginning, the time will help you to create one.

It's important also to do regular actions – daily or weekly for your goals. I have schedule that is created by my baby girl's life rhythm.

But I also set realistic goal and stick with it until I achieved it. For this book my goal was to work hard a month and now I fulfilled my plan. I feel content.

Another important thing is to not forget where and why you want to go. After that come the answers how you will do.

Thank you for reading!

About the Author's personality

The skills Victoria Mineva is proud of are: Organizing time, Get inspired by everyday situations, Finding joy in simple and small things, Being positive always, Making fast decisions, Balanced analyzing, Taking Actions, Supporting People, Chasing my dreams with persistence and Working good in hard situations.

As a person Victoria Mineva is Creative Writer, Business blogger,Self - Motivator, Inspirational Psychologist, Traveler, Autumn Lover, Wine admirer, Romanticist and Truthful to herself and her Friends.

The author has two published poetry books in Bulgarian online, one in English with a publisher "America Star Books" and a Kindle edition book for team building

If you wish to read more author's articles, follow these links:

http://victorydreamers.com – Bulgarian articles

http://victorydreamers.biz – English articles

http://www.amazon.com/Victoria-Mineva/eo/B0KJWTK8M - Books